LAUGHTER

THE BEST MEDICINE

JOKES FOR ADULTS

Billy Passione

Copyright page

ISBN No. 1479600

From the same author:

- **Ridere, la migliore medicina. Barzellette per adulti.** www.lulu.com or www.amazon.com (2008) [Italian]

Index

To my friends, to see them laugh

Introduction

Why this book?

Life is already too serious an affair to be taken seriously. I've been a doctor for over 20 years, and deal with life and death decisions on a daily basis. I always liked to write, and I wrote extensively in medicine. Now I feel the need to 'take a break', switch gear. I believe this book of jokes will also improve health, in fact directly improve the wellbeing of you readers, without intermediaries. Laughter increases secretion of catecholamines and of endorphins, increases oxygen in blood, relaxes arteries and so decreases blood pressure, and also increases the immune response.[1] I believe, and science proves it, that laughter is a wonderful medicine. It's important, no matter the circumstances, to keep some of our youth innocence. You do not quit playing because you become old; you become old because you quit playing.[2]

These jokes have been collected from private emails I received directly from friends in the last 10 years. I am a little embarrassed of these 'dirty' jokes, but I hope everybody will understand the spirit, and not get offended. Remember, I just collected them, I did not 'create' them, and I agree that some could be offensive, and I apologize ahead of time if you'll be insulted. On the other side, the beauty of a book is that it can be read in segret, without feeling shame, guilt, but, in this case, just for laughs. I'm far from ashamed: to look a fool is the secret of a wise man.[3] In fact I hope to get even closer in spirit to you, since it's said that laughter is the shortest distance between two people.

This book is dedicated to all my true and care-free friends who have sent me jokes via email, and to those of you who will fancy them.

Enjoy!

Billy Passione

[1]Robin Williams, in 'Patch Adams'; [2]Oliver Wendell Holmes; [3]Edgar Allan Poe *(as seen on the wall of Café' Regio, in New York City)*

Salary

When an efficient secretary asked her boss for a raise in her salary, he turned her down, saying: 'Your salary is already higher than that of the secretary at the next desk, and she has five children.'
'Excuse me,' the efficient woman replied, 'I thought we got paid for what we produce here – not for what we produce at home in our own time.'

Nudist Colony

A man moves into a nudist colony. He receives a letter from his mother asking him to send her a current photo of himself in his new location.
Too embarrassed to let her know that he lives in a nudist colony, he cuts a photo in half and sends her the top part.
Later he receives another letter asking him to send a picture to his grandmother.
The man cuts another picture in half, but accidentally sends the bottom half of the photo.
He is really worried when he realizes that he sent the wrong half, but then remembers how bad his grandmother's eyesight is, and hopes she won't notice.
A few weeks later he receives a letter from his grandmother.
It says.....
"Thank you for the picture. Change your hair style....it makes your nose look too short!"

Guilt

Howard had felt guilty all day long . No matter how much he tried to forget about it, he couldn't. The guilt and sense of shame was overwhelming, but, every once in a while, he'd hear that soothing voice trying to reassure him:
"Howard, don't worry about it. You're not the first doctor to sleep with one of your patients and you won't be the last. And, you're single. So, just let it go."
But, invariably the other voice would bring him back to reality........
"Howard, you're a veterinarian."

In the car

Late at night this guy runs into a pub and gets a glass of water from the bartender. The guy drinks it in one gulp then asks for a second glass. Six glasses later, and he has recovered enough to speak. "Thanks," he croaks.
"That's one hell of a thirst you've got," says the bartender.
The guy says, "Any man would be as bad if they'd just had sex with the woman in my car. She's insatiable. She wants me to go right back out there and do it all again, but I can't."
"Where's your car?" the landlord asks.
"At the roadside," the guy gasps.
"Tell you what," says the landlord, "you watch the bar for me while I go out and take your place."
"Be my guest, the broad's a nympo. She'll do anybody."
So the bartender goes outside and gets in the car. It's totally dark, so the woman doesn't realize she's with a different man. They get right down to it, humping away. Five minutes later there's a knock on the window. It's a cop and he shines his flashlight on the naked couple.
"What's going on here?" he asks.
"It's all right, officer," explains the bartender. "She's my wife."
"Oh, sorry sir, I didn't realize..."
"Neither did I till you switched on that damned light."

Olympics

A man is out shopping and discovers a new brand of Olympic Condoms.
Clearly impressed, he buys a pack. Upon getting home he announces to his wife the purchase he just made.
"Olympic condoms?", she blurts, "What makes them so special?"
"There are three colours", he replies, "Gold, Silver and Bronze."
"What colour are you going to wear tonight?", she asks cheekily.
"Gold of course", says the man proudly.
The wife responds, "Why don't you wear Silver? It would be nice if you came second for a change."

Golf

There's a fellow who is an avid golfer. Actually he's a golf fanatic.
Every Saturday morning he has an early tee time, gets up very early and golfs all day long.
Well this one Saturday morning, he gets up early, dresses quietly, gets his clubs out of the closet, and goes out to his car to drive to the course. It is raining a torrential downpour. There is snow mixed with the rain and the wind is blowing 50 mph.
He comes back into the house and turns the TV to the weather channel.
From there he finds it's going to be bad weather all day long.
So he puts his clubs back into the closet, quietly undresses and slips back into bed where he cuddles up to his wife's back, and whispers, "The weather out there is terrible." To which she replies, "Can you believe my stupid husband is out golfing?"

Nightmare

After a long night of making love, the young guy rolled over, pulled out a cigarette from his jeans and searched for his lighter.
Unable to find it, he asked the girl if she had one at hand.
"There might be some matches in the top drawer," she replied.
He opened the drawer of the bedside table and found a box of matches sitting neatly on top of a framed picture of another man. Naturally, the guy began to worry.
"Is this your husband?" he inquired nervously.
"No, silly," she replied, snuggling up to him.
"Your boyfriend then?" he asked.
"No, not at all," she said, nibbling away at his ear.
"Well, who is he then?" demanded the bewildered guy.
Calmly, the girl replied, "That's me before the operation."

Neutered

Overheard at the veterinarian's:
'I had my cat neutered. He's still out all night with the other cats, but now he's a consultant.'

Acronyms

Three guys and a lady were sitting at the bar talking about their professions. The first guy says: "I'm a Y.U.P.P.I.E, you know... Young, Urban,Professional, Peaceful, Intelligent, Ecologist."
The second guy says: "I'm a D.I.N.K.Y., you know ... Double Income, No Kids Yet."
The third guy says: "I'm a R.U.B., you know... Rich, Urban, Biker."
They turn to the woman and ask her: "What are you?"
She replies: "I'm a WIFE, you know ... Wash, Iron, Fuck, Etc."

MEN ARE LIKE ....

1. Men are like.....Laxatives.
They irritate the shit out of you.

2. Men are like......Bananas.
The older they get, the less firm they are.

3. Men are like.....Vacations.
They never seem to be long enough.

4. Men are like.....Bank Machines.
Once they withdraw they lose interest.

5. Men are like.....Weather.
Nothing can be done to change either one of them.

6. Men are like.....Blenders.
You need one, but you're not quite sure why.

7. Men are like.....Cement.
After getting laid, they take a long time to get hard.

8. Men are like.....Chocolate Bars.
Sweet, smooth, and they usually head right for your hips.

9. Men are like.....Coffee

The best ones are rich, warm, and can keep you up all night long.

10. Men are like.....Commercials.
You can't believe a word they say.

11. Men are like.....Department Stores.
Their clothes should always be half off.

12. Men are like.....Government bonds.
They take so long to mature.

13. Men are like.....Horoscopes.
They always tell you what to do and are usually wrong.

14. Men are like.....Lawn Mowers.
If you're not pushing one around, then you're riding it.

15. Men are like.....Mascara.
They usually run at the first sign of emotion.

16. Men are like.....Popcorn.
They satisfy you, but only for a little while.

17. Men are like.....Snowstorms.
You never know when he's coming, how many inches you'll get or how long he will last.

What is success?

At age 4, success is... not peeing in your pants
At age 12, success is... having friends
At age 20, success is... having sex
At age 35, success is... making money
At age 60, success is... having sex
At age 70, success is... having friends
At age 80, success is... not peeing in your pants

Social security

A retired gentleman went to the social security office to apply for Social security. After waiting in line a long time, he got to the counter.
The woman behind the counter asked him for his driver's license to verify his age.
He looked in his pockets and realised he had left his wallet at home.
He told the woman that he was very sorry, but he seemed to have left his wallet at home.
"I will have to go home and come back later."
The woman says, "Unbutton your shirt." So, he opens his shirt revealing lots of curly silver hair.
She says, "That silver hair on your chest is proof enough for me," and she processes his social security application.
When he gets home, the man excitedly tells his wife about his experience at the social security office.
She said, "You should have dropped your pants, you might have gotten disability benefit as well."

Sneeze

A man and a woman are riding next to each other in first class on a plane. The woman sneezes, then takes a tissue and gently wipes it between her legs.
The man isn't sure he saw what she did, and decides he is probably hallucinating.
A few minutes pass. The woman sneezes again.
She takes a tissue and gently wipes it between her legs.
The man is about to go nuts.
He can't believe that he's seeing what he's seeing.
A few more minutes pass. The woman sneezes yet again. She takes a tissue and gently wipes it between her legs yet again.
The man has finally had all he can handle. He turns to the woman and says: "Three times you've sneezed, and three times you've taken a tissue and wiped it between your legs! What kind of signals are you sending me, or are you just trying to drive me crazy?"
The woman replies: "I am sorry to have disturbed you, sir. I have a rare condition such that when I sneeze, I have an orgasm."
The man, now feeling badly, says, "Oh, I'm sorry. What are you taking for it?"
The woman looks at him and says,
"Pepper."

Things you can't explain

A farmer was sitting in the neighborhood bar getting drunk.
A man came in and asked the farmer, "Hey, why are you sitting here on this beautiful day, getting drunk?"
The farmer shook his head and replied, "Some things you just can't explain."
"So what happened that's so horrible?" the man asked as he sat down next to the farmer.
"Well," the farmer said, "today I was sitting by my cow, milking her. Just as I got the bucket full, she lifted her left leg and kicked over the bucket."
"Okay," said the man, "but that's not so bad."
"Some things you just can't explain," the farmer replied.
"So what happened then?" the man asked.
The farmer said: "I took her left leg and tied it to the post on the left."
"And then?"
"Well, I sat back down and continued to milk her. Just as I got the bucket full, she took her right leg and kicked over the bucket."
The man laughed and said: "Again?"
The farmer replied: "Some things you just can't explain."
"So, what did you do then?" the man asked.
"I took her right leg this time and tied it to the post on the right."
"And then?"
"Well, I sat back down and began milking her again. Just as I got the bucket full, the stupid cow knocked over the bucket with her tail."
"Hmmm," the man said and nodded his head.
"Some things you just can't explain," the farmer said.
"So, what did you do?" the man asked.
"Well," the farmer said, "I didn't have anymore rope, so I took off my belt and tied her tail to the rafter. In that moment, my pants fell down and my wife walked in ... Some things you just can't explain."

Toilet

15 Easy Steps To Crap Like A Woman:

1. Under no circumstances use any other toilet than your own, regardless of any stomach pain may be caused whilst waiting to get home.
2. With the toilet-brush, clean any residue left on the pan by your boyfriend/husband. Also wipe his pubes off the seat with some toilet paper.
3. Flush the toilet before starting. Then wash your hands.
4. Line the toilet seat with toilet paper (as other people may have sat on the toilet since it was last bleached).
5. Stuff toilet paper inside the pan to prevent splash-back.
6. Pull panties down and sit. Some women may still prefer to squat over the seat as opposed to taking the risk of touching it with bare flesh.
7. Release solids, but strain to avoid making any sounds.
8. Rise and quickly flush before direct eye-contact is made with any feces.
9. Take a length of toilet paper and fold it several times to positively guarantee that no residue will touch bare skin (about five or six applications per roll).
10. Wipe once and throw paper into the pan. Do not look at the paper.
11. Repeat steps 9 and 10 at least thirty times. It may be necessary to yell for your boyfriend/husband to find some more rolls to pass through the door while promising not to open his eyes or pass any comments. It is traditional to do this while he is trying to watch sport.
12. Flush the toilet and replace the lid.
13. Wash hands at least three times with disinfectant soap.
14. Open all windows and spray approximately half-a-can of air freshener.
15. Pick up all reading material left behind by your boyfriend/husband and leave bathroom, closing the door firmly behind you.

Ranking Order

The plane's cabin was being served by an obviously gay flight attendant who was just as obviously enjoying himself. He came swishing down the aisle and said through the PA: "Captain Marvey has asked me to announce that he'll be landing the big scary plane shortly, lovely people, so if you could just put up your trays that would be super."
On his trip back up the aisle, he noticed that one woman hadn't moved a muscle. "Perhaps you didn't hear me over those big brut you to raise your trazy-poo so the main man can pitty-pat us on the ground."
She calmly turned her head and said, "In my country, I am called a Princess. I take orders from no one." "Well, sweet-cheeks, in my country, I'm called a Queen, so I outrank you. Put the tray up, bitch."

Grandmother

The teenage granddaughter comes downstairs for her date with this see-through blouse on and no bra. Her grandmother just pitches a fit telling her not to dare go out like that!!!!
The teenager tells her, "Loosen up Grams. These are modern times. You gotta let your rosebuds show!" and out she goes.
The next day the teenager comes downstairs, and the grandmother is sitting there with no top on. The teenager wants to die. She explains to her Grandmother that she has friends coming over and that it just is not appropriate .....
The grandmother says, "Loosen up Sweetie. If you can show off your rosebuds, then I can display my hanging baskets."

Restaurant

A waitress walks up to one of her tables in a New York City restaurant and notices that the three Japanese businessmen seated there are furiously masturbating.
She yells, "What the hell do you guys think you are doing?"
One of the Japanese men explains, "Can't you see? We are all berry hungry."
The waitress begs the question, "So, how is whacking-off in the middle of the restaurant going to help that situation?"
One of the other Japanese men replies, "The menu says,
FIRST COME, FIRST SERVED!"

10 SIMPLE RULES FOR DATING MY DAUGHTER

Rule One: If you pull into my driveway and honk you'd better be delivering a package, because you're sure not picking anything up.

Rule Two: You do not touch my daughter in front of me. You may glance at her, so long as you do not peer at anything below her neck. If you cannot keep your eyes or hands off my daughter's body, I will remove them.

Rule Three: I am aware that it is considered fashionable for boys your age to wear their trousers so loosely that they appear to be falling off their hips. Please do not take this as an insult, but you and all of your friends are complete idiots. Still, I want to be fair and open minded about this issue, so I propose this compromise: You may come to the door with your underwear showing and your pants ten sizes too big, and I will object. However, in order to ensure that your clothes do not, in fact, come off during the course of your date with my daughter, I will take my electric nail gun and fasten your trousers securely in place to your waist.

Rule Four: I'm sure you've been told that in today's world sex without utilizing a "barrier method" of some kind will kill you. Let me elaborate: when it comes to sex, I am the barrier, and I will kill you.

Rule Five: In order for us to get to know each other, we should talk about sports, politics and other issues of the day. Please do not do this. The only information I require from you is an indication of when you expect to have my daughter safely back at my home, and the only word I need from you on this subject is "early".

Rule Six: I have no doubt you are a popular young fellow, with many opportunities to date other girls. This is fine with me as long as it is okay with my daughter. Otherwise, once you have gone out with my little girl, you will continue to date her until she is finished with you. If you make her cry, I will make you cry.

Rule Seven: As you stand in my front hallway, waiting for my daughter to appear, and more than an hour goes by, do not sigh and fidget. If you want to be on time for the movie, you should not be dating. My daughter is putting on her makeup, a process that can take longer than painting the Golden Gate Bridge. Instead of just standing there, why don't you do something useful, like changing the oil in my car.

Rule Eight: The following places are not appropriate for a date with my daughter: Places where there are beds, sofas, or anything softer than a wooden stool. Places where there are no parents, no policemen, or nuns within eyesight. Places where there is darkness. Places where there is dancing, holding hands, or happiness. Places where the ambient temperature is warm enough to induce my daughter to wear shorts, tank tops, midriff T-shirts, or anything other than overalls, a sweater, and a goose-down parka zipped up to her throat. Movies with strong romantic or sexual content in them are to be avoided; movies which feature chain saws are okay. Hockey games are okay. Old folks homes are better.

Rule Nine: Do not lie to me. I may appear to be a pot-bellied, balding, middle-aged, dim-witted has been. But on issues relating to my daughter, I am the all-knowing, merciless god of your universe. If I ask you where you are going and with whom, you have one chance to tell me the truth. I have a shotgun, a shovel, and five acres behind the house. Do not mess with me.

Rule Ten: Be afraid. Be very afraid. It takes very little for me to mistake the sound of your car in the driveway for a chopper coming in over a rice paddy outside Hanoi. When my Agent Orange starts acting up, the voices in my head frequently tell me to clean the guns as I wait for you to bring my daughter home. As you pull into the driveway you should exit the car with both hands in sight. Speak the perimeter password, announce in a clear voice that you have brought my daughter home safely and early, then return to you car - there is no need for you to come inside. The camouflaged face in the window is mine.

Flowers

Two friends, a blonde and a brunette, are walking down the street and pass a flower shop where the brunette happens to see her boyfriend buying flowers.
She sighs and says, "Oh, crap, my boyfriend is buying me flowers again...for no reason."
The blonde looks quizzically at her and says, "What's the big deal, don't you like getting flowers?"
The brunette says, "Oh sure... but he always has expectations after getting me flowers, and I just don't feel like spending the next three days on my back with my legs in the air."
The blonde says, ..."Don't you have a vase?

Lifesavers' names

A man was doing a study of children's senses in a first-grade class using a bowl of Lifesavers. He would ask them to identify the color and then the flavor as they tasted the Lifesavers. The children began to say,
"Red...cherry"
"Yellow...lemon"
"Green...lime"
"Orange...orange"
Finally he gave them all honey flavored Lifesavers.
The children sucked on them for a while, but they couldn't decipher the taste.
"Well," he said, "I'll give you a clue. It's what your mother would call your father!"
One little girl looked up in horror.
She quickly spit the Lifesaver out and shouted: "Everybody, spit it out. They're assholes!"

Bad doggies

Three dogs were sitting in the waiting room at the veterinarian's.
One of the dogs was hanging its head and sighing.
The second dog turned to him and asked: "What are you in here for, buddy?"
The dog looked depressed, "I'm in big trouble," he said. "My owner has a really nice sports car with leather seats and I just love to go for rides in it. Well, the other day, he took me for a ride and I was so excited, I peed on the nice leather seat. Now he's having me put to sleep."
"I know how you feel," said the second dog. "My owners have a beautiful, expensive oriental rug. The other day they were late getting home from work and I just couldn't help myself...I shit all over their nice carpet and ruined it. They're having me put to sleep, too."
Both dogs turned to the third dog in the waiting room. "So what are you here for?" they asked.
"Well," said the third dog, "my owner likes to do her housework in the nude. The other day, she was vacuuming and she knelt down to vacuum under the sofa, and I just couldn't help myself. I hopped on her back and had the ride of my life!"
The other dogs nodded in sympathy, "So she's having you put to sleep, too, huh?"
"No," said the dog, "I'm having my nails clipped."

Convicts

Three international convicts were on the way to prison. They were each allowed to take one item with them to help occupy their time while incarcerated.
On the bus, one turned to another and said: "So, what did you bring?"
The French convict pulled out a box of paints and stated that he intended to paint anything he could. He wanted to become the "Claude Monet of prison."
Then he asked the first: "What did you bring?"
The Israeli convict pulled out a deck of cards and said: "I brought cards. I can play poker, solitaire and gin, and any number of games."
The third convict was sitting quietly aside, grinning to himself.
The other two took notice and asked: "Why are you so smug? What did you bring?"
The Irish convict pulled out a box of tampons and smiled. He said: "I brought these."
The other two were puzzled and asked: "What can you do with those?"
He grinned and pointed to the box and said, "Well, according to this,
I can go horseback riding, swimming, roller-skating . . ."

JEWISH OR BLACK?

Little Johnny came home from school one day slightly confused.
His mother was Jewish and his father was black.
So Johnny says:
"Mum, am I more Jewish or more black?"
"What does it really matter? You'll just have to ask your father", his mother tells him.
So Johnny's father gets home from work and Johnny asks the same question,
"Dad, am I more Jewish or more black?"
"What kind of a question is that, does it really matter? Why do you want to know if you're more Jewish or black?" asks his dad.
"Well, it's like this dad. Tommy down the street wants to sell his bicycle for $50, I don't know whether to talk him down to $25, or wait till its dark and steal the fucking thing."

Logic

Two rednecks decided that they weren't going anywhere in life and thought they should go to college to get ahead. The first went in to see the counselor, who told him to take math, history, and logic.

"What's logic?" the first redneck asked.

The professor answered, "Let me give you an example. Do you own a weed eater?"

"I sure do."

"Then I can assume, using logic, that you have a yard," replied the professor.

"That's real good!" said the redneck.

The professor continued, "Logic will also tell me that since you have a yard, you also own a house."

Impressed, the redneck said, "Amazing!"

"And since you own a house, logic dictates that you have a wife."

"That's Betty Mae! This is incredible!" The redneck was catching on.

"Finally, since you have a wife, logically I can assume that you are heterosexual," said the professor.

"You're absolutely right! Why that's the most fascinating thing I ever heard! I can't wait to take that logic class!"

The redneck, proud of the new world opening up to him, walked back into the hallway where his friend was still waiting.

"So what classes are ya takin' ?" asked the friend.

"Math, history, and logic!" replied the first redneck.

"What in tarnation is logic?" asked his friend.

"Let me give you an example. Do ya own a weed eater?" asked the first redneck.

"No," his friend replied.

"You're queer, ain't ya?"

Age

A woman decided to have a face lift for her birthday. She spent $5000 and felt really good about the results. On her way home she stopped at a dress shop to look around. As she was leaving, she said to the sales clerk: "I hope you don't mind me asking, but how old do you think I am?"
"About 35," was the reply.
"I'm actually 47," the woman said, feeling really happy.
After that she went into McDonalds for lunch and asked the order taker the same question.
He replied, "Oh, you look about 29."
"I am actually 47!" she said, feeling really good.
While standing at the bus stop she asked an old man the same question. He replied: "I am 85 years old and my eyesight is going. But when I was young there was a sure way of telling a woman's age. If I put my hand up your skirt I will be able to tell your exact age."
There was no one around, so the woman said, "What the hell?" and let him slip his hand up her skirt.
After feeling around for a while, the old man said, "OK, You are 47."
Stunned, the woman said, "That was brilliant! How did you do that?"
The old man replied, "I was behind you in line at McDonalds."

Gynecologist

A beautiful woman went to a gynecologist. The doctor took one look at this woman and all his professionalism went out the window. He immediately told her to undress. After she had disrobed, the doctor began to stroke her thigh. Doing so, he asked her, "Do you know what I'm doing?"
"Yes," she replied, "you're checking for any abrasions or dermatological abnormalities."
"That is right," said the doctor. He then began to fondle her breasts.
"Do you know what I'm doing now?" he asked.
"Yes," the woman said, "you're checking for any lumps or breast cancer."
"Correct," replied the shady doctor. Finally, he mounted his patient and started having sexual intercourse with her. He asked, "Do you know what I'm doing now?"
"Yes," she said. "You're getting herpes, which is why I came here in the first place."

Nun

A cabbie picks up a nun. She gets into the cab, and the cab driver won't stop staring at her. She asks him why is he staring and he replies, "I have a question to ask you but I don't want to offend you."
She answers, "My dear son, you cannot offend me. When you're as old as I am and have been a nun as long as I have, you get a chance to see and hear just about everything. I'm sure that there's nothing you could say or ask that I would find offensive."
"Well, I've always had a fantasy to have a nun kiss me."
She responds: "Well, let's see what we can do about that: #1. you have to be single, and #2. you must be Catholic."
The cab driver is very excited and says, "Yes, I am single and I'm Catholic too!"
"OK" the nun says "Pull into the next alley."
He does and the nun fulfils his fantasy with a kiss that would make a hooker blush.
But when they get back on the road, the cab driver starts crying.
"My dear child, said the nun, why are you crying?"
"Forgive me sister, but I have sinned. I lied, I must confess, I'm married and I'm Jewish."
The nun says, "That's OK, my name is Kevin and I'm on my way to a Halloween party."

How to impress

HOW TO IMPRESS A WOMAN
Wine her,
Dine her,
Call her,
Hug her,
Support her,
Hold her,
Surprise her,
Compliment her,
Smile at her,
Listen to her,
Laugh with her,
Cry with her,
Romance her,

Believe in her,
Cuddle with her,
Shop with her,
Give her jewelry,
Buy her flowers,
Hold her hand,
Write love letters to her,
Go to the end of the earth and back again for her.

HOW TO IMPRESS A MAN
Show up naked.
Bring food.

Politics

This little boy goes to his Dad and asks: "What is politics?"
Dad says: "Well, son, let me try to explain it to you this way...I'm the breadwinner of the family, so let's call me 'Capitalism'. Your Mom, she's the administrator of the household, so we'll call her the 'Government'. We're here to take care of YOUR needs, so we'll call you 'The People'. The nanny, well, she works hard all day for very little money, so we'll consider her 'The Working Class'. And, your baby brother...we'll call him 'The Future'. Now, think about that and see if it makes sense."
So, the little boy goes off to bed thinking about what his Dad had said.
Later that night, he hears his baby brother crying, so he gets up to check on him.
He finds that the baby has severely soiled this diaper...big time!
The little boy goes to his parents' room and finds his mother sound asleep.
Not wanting to wake her, he goes to the nanny's room. Finding the door locked, he peeks into the keyhole and sees his father in bed with the nanny.
He gives up and goes back to bed.
The next morning, the little boy says to his father, "Dad, I think I understand the concept of politics now."
The father says, "Good, son, tell me, in your own words, what you think politics is all about."
The little boy replies, "Well, while Capitalism is screwing The Working Class, the Government is sound asleep, The People are being ignored, and The Future is in Deep Shit."

Hail to the Redskins!!!

Barbara Walters was doing a documentary on the customs of American Indians. While touring a reservation during the documentary, she was puzzled as to why the difference in the number of feathers in the headdresses. So she asked a brave who only had one feather in his headdress and his reply was:
"Me have only one squaw, me only have one feather."
Feeling the first fellow was only joking, she asked another brave. This brave had four feathers in his headdress. And he replied: "Ugh, me have four feathers because me sleep with four squaw."
Still not convinced the feathers indicated the number of squaws involved, she decided to interview the Chief. Now the Chief had a headdress full of feathers. Which, needless to say, amused Ms. Walters.
She asked the Chief, "Why do you have so many feathers in your headdress?"
The Chief proudly pounded his chest and said:
"Me Chief, me sleep with 'em all. Big, small, fat and tall, me sleep with 'em all."
Horrified, Ms. Walters stated, "You ought to be hung."
The Chief replied: "You damn right, me hung, big like buffalo, long like snake."
Ms. Walters cried, "You don't have to be so hostile."
The Chief replied:
"Hoss-style, dog-style, wolf-style, any style me sleep with 'em all."
With tears in her eyes, Ms. Walters cried, "Oh dear"
The Chief said: "No deer. Ass too high, run too fast."

Australian Tourism Website Queries

Three Aussie tourism staff have been recently reprimanded for their responses to email tourist questions - wonder why?

Q: I was in Australia in 1969 on R+R, and I want to contact the girl I dated while I was staying in Kings Cross. Can you help? (USA)
A: Yes, and you will still have to pay her by the hour.

Q: Can you tell me the regions in Tasmania where the female population is smaller than the male population? (Italy)
A: Yes, gay nightclubs.

Embarrassing Moments

Curl Up and Die
I walked into a hair salon with my husband and three kids in tow and asked loudly, "How much do you charge for a shampoo and a blow job?"

Pad, please!
An insurance man visited me at home to talk about our mortgage insurance. He was throwing a lot of facts and figures at me, and I wanted to follow as best I could, so I told my 6-year-old son to run and get me a pad. He came back and handed me a Kotex right in front of our guest.

Ho, Ho, Ho
I was taking a shower when my 2-year-old son came into the bathroom and wrapped himself in toilet paper. Although he made a mess, he looked adorable, so I ran for my camera and took a few shots. They came out so well that I had copies made and included one with each of our Christmas cards. Days later, a relative called about the picture, laughing hysterically, and suggesting I take a closer look. Puzzled, I stared at the photo and was shocked to discover that in addition to my son, I had captured my reflection in the mirror - wearing nothing but a camera!

Lady Golfer
I was at the golf store comparing different kinds of golf balls. I was unhappy with the women's type I had been using. After browsing for several minutes, I was approached by one of the good looking gentlemen who works at the store. He asked if he could help me. Without thinking, I looked at him and said, "I think I like playing with men's balls."

Nuts about You
My sister and I were at the mall and passed by a store that sold a variety of nuts. As we were looking at the display case, the boy behind the counter asked if we needed any help. I replied, "No, I'm just looking at your nuts." My sister started to laugh hysterically, the boy grinned, and I turned beet-red and walked away. To this day, my sister has never let me forget.

The following are the top four winners of a Most Embarrassing Moments Contest in the New Woman Magazine":

Na-na na-na na-nah!
While in line at the bank one afternoon, my toddler decided to release some pent-up energy and ran amok. I was finally able to grab hold of her after receiving looks of disgust and annoyance from other patrons. I told her that if she did not start behaving "right now" she would be punished. To my horror, she looked me in the eye and said in a voice just as threatening, "If you don't let me go right now, I will tell Grandma that I saw you kissing Daddy's pee-pee last night!" The silence was deafening after this enlightening exchange. Even the tellers stopped what they were doing. I mustered up the last of my dignity and walked out of the bank with my daughter in tow. The last thing I heard when the door closed behind me were screams of laughter.

Surprise!
It was the day before my eighteenth birthday. I was living at home, but my parents had gone out for the evening, so I invited my girlfriend over for a romantic night alone. As we lay in bed after making love, we heard the telephone ring downstairs. I suggested to my girlfriend that I give her a nude piggyback ride to the phone. Since we didn't want to miss the call, we didn't have time to get dressed. When we got to the bottom of the stairs, the lights suddenly came on and a whole crowd of people yelled, "SURPRISE!" My entire family: aunts, uncles, grandparents, cousins and all my friends were standing there. My girlfriend and I were frozen in a state of shock and embarrassment for what seemed like an eternity. Since then, no one in my family has planned a surprise party again.

Priceless
One of the funniest "most-embarrassing-moment" stories I've come upon in a long time was about a lady who picked up several items at a discount store. When she finally got up to the checker, she learned that one of her items had no price tag. Imagine her embarrassment when the checker got on the intercom and boomed out for all the store to hear, "PRICE CHECK ON LANE THIRTEEN, TAMPAX, SUPER SIZE." That was bad enough, but somebody at the rear of the store apparently misunderstood the word "Tampax" for "THUMBTACKS." In a business-like tone, a voice boomed back over the intercom. "DO YOU WANT THE KIND YOU PUSH IN WITH YOUR THUMB OR THE KIND YOU POUND IN WITH A HAMMER?"

Mom's Advice
A teacher noticed that a little boy at the back of the class was squirming around, scratching his crotch and not paying attention. She went back to find out what was going on. He was quite embarrassed and whispered that he had just recently been circumcised and he was quite itchy. The teacher told him to go down to the principal's office. He was to phone his mother and ask her what he should do about it. He did it and returned to his class. Suddenly, there was a commotion at the back of the room. She went back to investigate only to find him sitting at his desk with his penis hanging out.
"I thought I told you to call your mom," she screamed.
"I did," he said," and she told me that if I could stick it out till noon, she'd come and pick me up from school."

Consequences

There was a fly flying 6 inches above a lake.
A fish in the lake thinks, "If that fly dropped 6 inches I'd get it!"
A bear on land thinks, "If that fly dropped 6 inches, the fish would jump out of the water, and I'd get it!"
A hunter thinks, "If that fly drops 6 inches, the fish would jump, the bear will go to get the fish, and I'll shoot the bear."
A mouse thinks, "If that fly drops 6 inches, the fish would jump, the bear would go to get the fish, the hunter will go to get the bear, and I'll steal the cheese off his sandwich!"
A cat thinks, "If that fly drops 6 inches, the fish would jump, the bear would go to get the fish, the hunter will go to get the bear, the mouse will go get the cheese, and I'll get that mouse!!!"
Suddenly, it all happened:
The fly dropped 6 inches, the fish got the fly, the bear got the fish, the hunter got the bear, the mouse got the hunter's cheese, but the cat missed the mouse and fell in the water!!!!!
The Moral Of This Story Is..................
"Everytime time a fly drops 6 inches, a pussy gets wet!!!

Barber

A guy sticks his head into a barber shop and asks,
"How long before I can get a haircut?"
The barber looks around the shop and says, "About 2 hours."
The guy leaves.
A few days later the same guy sticks his head in the door and asks,
"How long before I can get a haircut?"
The barber looks around at the shop full of customers and says, "About 3 hours."
The guy leaves.
A week later the same guy sticks his head in the shop and asks,"How long before I can get a haircut?"
The barber looks around the shop and says, "About an hour and a half."
The guy leaves.
The barber looks over at a friend in the shop and says, "Hey, Bill. Follow that guy and see where he goes. "
A little while later, Bill comes back into the shop, laughing hysterically.
The barber ask, "Bill, where did he go when he left here?"
Bill looks up, tears in his eyes and says," Your house."

Check-up

A 75 year old woman went to the doctor for a check-up.
The doctor told her she needed more activity and recommended sex three times a week.
She said to the doctor, "Please, tell my husband."
The doctor walked into the waiting room and told her husband that his wife needed to have sex three times a week.
The 80 year old husband replied, "Which days?"
The doctor answered, "How about Monday, Wednesday and Friday."
The husband said, "I can bring her Monday and Wednesday, but on Fridays, she'll have to take the bus."

Perfect day

PERFECT DAY FOR A WOMAN:
8:15 Wake up to hugs and kisses.
8:30 Weigh 5 lbs. lighter than yesterday.
8:45 Breakfast in bed, fresh squeezed orange juice and croissants.
9.15 Soothing hot bath with fragrant lilac bath oil.
10:00 Light workout at club with handsome, funny personal trainer.
10:30 Facial, manicure, shampoo, and comb out.
12:00 Lunch with best friend at an outdoor cafe.
12:45 Notice ex-boyfriend's wife, she has gained 30 lbs.
1:00 Shopping with friends.
3:00 Nap.
4:00 A dozen roses delivered by florist. Card is from a secret admirer.
4:15 Light workout at club followed by a gentle massage.
5:30 Pick outfit for dinner. Primp before mirror.
7:30 Candlelight dinner for two followed by dancing.
10:00 Hot shower. Alone.
10:30 Make love.
11:00 Pillow talk, light touching and cuddling.
11:15 Fall asleep in his big, strong arms.

PERFECT DAY FOR A MAN:
6:00 Alarm.
6:15 Blowjob.
6:30 Massive dump while reading the sports section.
7:00 Breakfast. Filet Mignon, eggs, toast and coffee.
7:30 Limo arrives.
7:45 Bloody Mary en route to airport.
9:30 Limo to Augusta National Golf Club.
9:45 Play front nine at Augusta, finish 2 under par.
11:45 Lunch. 2 dozen oysters on the half shell. 3 Heinekens.
12:15 Blowjob.
12:30 Play back nine at Augusta, finish 4 under par.
2:15 Limo back to airport. Drink 2 Bombay martinis.
2:30 Private jet to Nassau, Bahamas. Nap.
3:15 Late afternoon fishing excursion with topless female crew.
4:30 Catch world record light-tackle marlin-1249 lbs.
4:45 Play in the dirt with a Bobcat making holes and then burying them.

5:00 Jet back home. En route, get massage from naked supermodel.
7:00 Watch Sportscenter.
7:30 Dinner. Lobster appetizers, 1963 Dom Perignon, 20 Oz. New York strip steak.
9:00 Relax after dinner with 1789 Augler Cognac and Cohiba Cuban cigar.
10:00 Have sex with two 18 year old nymphomaniacs.
11:00 Massage and Jacuzzi.
11:45 Go to bed.
11:50 Let loose a 12 second, 4 octave fart. Watch the dog leave the room.
11:55 Laugh yourself to sleep.

Secret

When Bill and Hillary first got married, Bill said, "I am putting a box under the bed. You must promise never to look in it."

In all their 25 years of marriage Hillary never looked. However, on the afternoon of their 25th anniversary, curiosity got the best of her and she lifted the lid and peeked inside.

In the box were 3 empty beer cans and $81,874.25 in cash.

She closed the box and put it back under the bed. Now that she knew what was in the box, she was doubly curious as to why. That evening they were out for a special dinner.

After dinner, Hillary could no longer contain her curiosity and she confessed, saying, "I am so sorry. For all these years I kept my promise and never looked into the box under the bed. However, today the temptation was too much and I gave in. But now I need to know, why do you keep the cans in the box?"

Bill thought for a while and said, "I guess after all these years you deserve to know the truth. Whenever I was unfaithful to you, I put an empty beer can in the box under the bed to remind myself not to do it again."

Hillary was shocked, but said, "Hmmmmm, Jennifer, Paula and Monica.
I am very disappointed and saddened but temptation does happen and I guess that 3 times is not that bad considering the years."

They hugged and made their peace. A little while later Hillary asked Bill, "So why do you have all that money in the box?"

Bill answered, "Well, whenever the box filled up with empty cans, I took them to the recycling center and redeemed them for cash."

Dark in here

A women takes a lover during the day, while her husband is at work. Her 9 year old son comes home unexpectedly, so she puts him in the closet and shuts the door. Her husband also comes home, so she puts her lover in the closet, with the little boy. The little boy says, "Dark in here." The man says, "Yes, it is."
Boy - "I have a baseball."
Man - "That's nice."
Boy - "Want to buy it?"
Man - "No, thanks."
Boy - "My dad's outside."
Man - "OK, how much?"
Boy - "$250"
In the next few weeks, it happens again that the boy and the lover are in the closet together.
Boy - "Dark in here."
Man - "Yes, it is."
Boy - "I have a baseball glove."
The lover, remembering the last time, asks the boy, "How much?"
Boy - "$750"
Man - "Fine."
A few days later, the father says to the boy "Grab your glove. Let's go outside and toss the baseball back and forth."
The boy says, "I can't, I sold them."
The father asks, "How much did you sell them for?"
Boy - "$1,000"
The father says, "That's terrible to overcharge your friends like that. That is way more than those two things cost. I'm going to take you to church and make you confess."
They go to the church and the father makes the little boy sit in the confession booth and he closes the door.
The boy says, "Dark in here."
The priest says, "Don't start that again."

Parrot

A guy decides that maybe he'd like to have a pet and goes to a petshop.
After looking around he spots a parrot sitting on a little perch; it doesn't have any feet or legs.
The guy says out loud, "Geez, I wonder what happened to this parrot?"
“I was born this way," says the parrot. "I'm a defective parrot."
Ha, ha," the guy laughs. "It sounded like this parrot actually understood what I said and answered me."
I understand every word," says the parrot. "I am a highly intelligent and thoroughly educated bird."
"Yeah?" the guy asks. "Then answer this: how do you hang onto your perch without any feet?"
"Well," the parrot says, "this is a little embarrassing, but since you asked, I will tell you. I wrap my little parrot penis around this wooden bar, kind of like a little hook. You can't see it because of my feathers."
"Wow," says the guy, "you really can understand and answer; can't you?"
"Of course. I speak both Spanish and English. I can converse with reasonable competence on almost any subject: politics, religion, sports, physics, philosophy. And I am especially good at ornithology.
You should buy me; I am a great companion."
The guy looks at the $200.00 price tag. He says. "I can't afford that."
"Pssst," the parrot hisses, motioning the guy over with one wing.
"Nobody wants me because I don't have any feet. You can get me for $20.00; just make an offer."
The guy offers twenty dollars and walks out with the parrot.
Weeks go by and the parrot is sensational.
He's funny; he's interesting; he's a great pal, he understands everything, sympathizes, and gives good advice. The guy is delighted.
One day the guy comes home from work and the parrot says, "Pssst," and motions him over with one wing. The guy goes up close to the cage.
"I don't know if I should tell you this or not," says the parrot, "but it's about your wife and the mailman."
"What?" asks the guy.
"Well," the parrot says, "when the mailman came to the door today, your wife greeted him in a sheer nightgown and kissed him on the mouth."
"What happened then?" asks the guy.
"Then the mailman came into the house and lifted up the nightgown and began petting her all over," reports the parrot.

"My God!" the guy says. "Then what?"
"Then he lifted up the nightgown, got down on his knees and began to lick her body, starting with her breasts slowly going down and down."
The parrot pauses for a long time...
"What happened? What happened?" says the frantic guy.
"I don't know," says the Parrot, "I got a hard-on and I fell off my perch."

He said... She said...

He said... Want a quickie?
She said... As opposed to what?

He said... I don't know why you wear a bra; you've got nothing to put in it.
She said...You wear briefs, don't you?

He said... Do you love me just because my father left me a fortune?
She said... Not at all honey, I would love you no matter who left you the money.

She said... I won the lottery! Five million dollars. Whoo-ee, start packing!
He said... That's great!!! What should I pack?
She said...Whatever you want, just be out of the house by the time I get there.

He said... This coffee isn't fit for a pig!
She said... No problem, I'll get you some that is.

She said... What do you mean by coming home half drunk?
He said... It's not my fault...I ran out of money.

He said... Since I first laid eyes on you, I've wanted to make love to you in the worst way.
She said... Well, you succeeded.

He said... If you only could learn to make me a proper meal, then we could manage without the cook. And if you cleaned the house, we could fire the maid as well.
She said... Darling, if you only could learn to satisfy me properly we could do without the gardener too.

Priest... I don't think you will ever find another man like your late husband.
She said... Who's gonna look?

He said... You have a flat chest and need to shave your legs, have you ever been mistaken for a man?
She said... No, have you?

He said... Why do you women always try to impress us with your looks, not with your brains?
She said... Because there is a bigger chance that a man is a moron than he is blind.

He said... What have you been doing with all the grocery money I gave you?
She said... Turn sideways and look in the mirror.

He said... Let's go out and have some fun tonight.
She said... Okay, but if you get home before I do, leave the hallway light on.

Honeymoon

A guy out on the golf course took a high speed ball right in the crotch. Writhing in agony, he fell to the ground. He finally got himself to the doctor.
He said, "How bad is it doc? I'm going on my honeymoon next week and my fiance is still a virgin in everyway."
The doc said, "I'll have to put your penis in a splint to let it heal and keep it straight. It should be okay next week."
So he took four tongue depressors and formed a neat little 4-sided bandage and wired it all together. It was an impressive work of art.
The guy mentioned none of this to his girlfriend. They married and on their honeymoon night in the motel room, she ripped open her blouse to reveal a gorgeous set of breasts. This was the first time he ever saw them.
She said, "You are the first, no one has ever touched these breasts."
He pulled down his pants, whipped it out and said......
"Look at this, it's still in the crate!"

On the train

A man and a woman who have never met before find themselves assigned to the same sleeping room on a transcontinental train. After the initial embarrassment and uneasiness, they both go to sleep, the man in the upper berth, and the woman in the lower berth.
In the middle of the night the man leans over, wakes the woman and says:
"I'm sorry to bother you, but I'm awfully cold and I was wondering if you could possibly reach over and get me another blanket?"
The woman leans out and, with a glint in her eye, says:
"I have a better idea. Just for tonight let's pretend that we are married."
The man happily says: "OK. Brilliant!"
The woman says: "Good ... get your own blanket."

SOMETHING TO OFFEND DAMN-NEAR EVERYBODY

What's the Cuban national anthem?
Row, Row, Row Your Boat"

Where does an Irish family go on vacation?
A different bar.

Did you hear about the Chinese couple that had a retarded baby?
They named him "Sum Ting Wong."

What would you call it when an Italian has one arm shorter than the other?
A speech impediment.

What does it mean when the flag at the Post Office is flying at half mast?
They're hiring.

Why aren't there any Puerto Ricans on Star Trek?
Because they're not going to work in the future, either.

What do you call an Alabama farmer with a sheep under each arm?
A pimp.

What's the difference between a southern zoo and a northern zoo?
A southern zoo has a description of the animal on the front of the cage, along with a recipe.

What's the difference between a northern fairytale and a southern fairytale?
A northern fairytale begins "Once upon a time..."
A southern fairytale begins 'Y'all ain't gonna believe this shit..."

Times have changed. Years ago.....When 100 white men chased 1 black man, we called it the Ku Klux Klan. Today, they call it the PGA TOUR.

Who is Jack Schitt?

For some time many of us have wondered just who is Jack Schitt?
We find ourselves at a loss when someone says, "You don't know Jack Schitt!"
Well, thanks to my genealogy efforts, you can now respond in an intellectual way.
Jack Schitt is the only son of Awe Schitt. Awe Schitt, the fertilizer magnate, married O. Schitt, the owner of Needeep N. Schitt, Inc.
They had one son, Jack.
In turn, Jack Schitt married Noe Schitt.
The deeply religious couple produced six children: Holie Schitt, Giva Schitt, Fulla Schitt, Bull Schitt, and the twins Deap Schitt and Dip Schitt.
Against her parents' objections, Deap Schitt married Dumb Schitt, a high school dropout.
After being married 15 years, Jack and Noe Schitt divorced. Noe Schitt later married Ted Sherlock, and, because her kids were living with them, she wanted to keep her previous name. She was then known as Noe Schitt Sherlock.
Meanwhile, Dip Schitt married Loda Schitt, and they produced a son with a rather nervous disposition named Chicken Schitt.
Two of the other six children, Fulla Schitt and Giva Schitt, were inseparable throughout childhood and subsequently married the Happens brothers in a dual ceremony. The wedding announcement in the newspaper was the Schitt-Happens nuptials. The Schitt-Happens children were Dawg, Byrd, and Hoarse.
Bull Schitt, the prodigal son, left home to tour the world.
He recently returned from Italy with his new Italian bride, Pisa Schitt.
Now when someone says, "You don't know Jack Schitt," you can correct them.
Sincerely,
Crock O. Schitt

Young again

A naked woman is bouncing on her bed singing.
Her husband walks into the bedroom and sees her.
He watches her a for a while, then says, "You look ridiculous! What on earth do you think you're doing?"
She says, "I just got my checkup and my doctor says I have the breasts of an eighteen year old."
She starts laughing and jumping again.
He says, "Yeah, right. And what did he say about your 45-year-old ass?"
"Your name never came up," she replied.

Obsessions

A psychiatrist was conducting a group therapy session with four young mothers and their small children.
"You all have obsessions," he observed. To the first mother, he said, "You are obsessed with eating. You've even named your daughter Candy."
He turned to the second mom. "Your obsession is money. Again, it manifests itself in your child's name, Penny."
He turned to the third mom. "Your obsession is alcohol. Again, it manifests itself in your child's name, Brandy."
At this point, the fourth mother got up, took her little boy by the hand and whispered, "Come on, Dick, let's go..."

What to do with Osama bin Laden

Killing him will only create a martyr.
Holding him prisoner will inspire his comrades to take hostages to demand his release.
Therefore, I suggest we do neither.
Let the Special Forces, Seals or whatever covertly capture him, fly him to an undisclosed hospital and have surgeons quickly perform a complete sex change operation.
Then, we return "her" to Afghanistan to live as a woman under the Taliban.

Who said that?

It was the first day of school and a new student named Suzuki, the son of a Japanese businessman, entered the fourth grade.
The teacher said, "Let's begin by reviewing some American history.
Who said 'Give me Liberty, or give me Death?'"
She saw a sea of blank faces, except for Suzuki, who had his hand up.
"Patrick Henry, 1775," he said.
"Very good! Who said 'Government of the people, by the people, for the people, shall not perish from the earth'"?
Again, no response except from Suzuki:
"Abraham Lincoln, 1863," said Suzuki.
The teacher snapped at the class, "Class, you should be ashamed. Suzuki, who is new to our country, knows more about its history than you do."
She heard a loud whisper: "Fuck the Japs."
"Who said that?" she demanded.
Suzuki put his hand up. "Lee Iacocca, 1982."
At that point, a student in the back said, "I'm gonna puke."
The teacher glares and asks "All right! Now, who said that?"
Again, Suzuki says, "George Bush to the Japanese Prime Minister, 1991."
Now furious, another student yells, "Oh yeah? Suck this!"
Suzuki jumps out of his chair waving his hand and shouts to the teacher, "Bill Clinton, to Monica Lewinsky, 1997!"
Now with almost a mob hysteria someone said, "You little shit. If you say anything else, I'll kill you."
Suzuki frantically yells at the top of his voice, "Gary Condit to Chandra Levy 2001."
The teacher fainted.

Misunderstanding

For his birthday Little Johnny asked for a 10 speed bicycle. His father said, "Son, we'd love to give you a bicycle, but the mortgage on this house is $80,000 and your mother just lost her job. There's no way we can afford it."
The next day the father saw Little Johnny heading out the front door with a suitcase. So he asked, "Son, where are you going?"
Little Johnny told him, "I was walking past your room last night and I heard you tell Mom you were pulling out. I heard her tell you to wait because she was coming too. And I'll be damned if I'm sticking around here by myself with an $80,000 mortgage and no transportation."

Art

A couple is attending an Art exhibit and they are looking at a portrait that has them a little taken aback. The picture depicts 3 very black, very naked men sitting on a park bench; 2 have a black penis and the one in the middle has a pink penis.
As the couple is looking somewhat puzzled at the picture, the Irish artist walks by and says, "Can I help you with this painting? I'm the artist who painted it."
The man says: "Well, we like the painting but don't understand why you have 3 African men on a bench, and the one in the middle has a pink penis, while the other two have a black penis."
The Irish artist says, "Oh you are misinterpreting the painting.
They're not African men, they are Irish coal miners and the one in the middle went home for lunch."

Famous phrases by Woody Allen

“My wife is a sex object. Every time I ask for sex, she objects."

“I believe that sex is a beautiful thing between two people.
Between five, it's fantastic."

“If there is reincarnation, I'd like to come back as Pamela Anderson's fingertips."

“I'm such a good lover because I practice a lot on my own."

“My love life is terrible. The last time I was inside a woman was when I visited the Statue of Liberty."

Phrases

"See, the problem is that God gives men a brain and a penis, and only enough blood to run one at a time."
Robin Williams

"What do people mean when they say the computer went down on them?"
Marilyn Pittman

"Bigamy is having one spouse too many. Monogamy is the same."
Oscar Wilde

"Suppose you were an idiot . . . . And suppose you were a member of Congress ... . . . But I repeat myself."
Mark Twain

"Ah, yes, divorce......., from the Latin word meaning to rip out a man's genitals through his wallet."
Robin Williams

"Women need a reason to have sex. Men just need a place."
Billy Crystal

Do you know why they call it "PMS"? Because " Mad Cow Disease" was taken.
Unknown, presumed deceased

Sister-in-law

I was happy. My girlfriend and I had been dating for over a year, and so we decided to get married. My parents helped us in every way, my friends encouraged me, and my girlfriend? She was a dream!

There was only one thing bothering me, very much indeed, and that one thing was her younger sister. My prospective sister-in-law was twenty years of age, wore tight mini skirts and low cut blouses. She would regularly bend down when quite near me and I got many a pleasant view of her underwear.

It had to be deliberate. She never did it when she was near anyone else.

One day little sister called and asked me to come over to check the wedding invitations. She was alone when I arrived. She whispered to me that soon I was to be married, and she had feelings and desires for me that she couldn't overcome and didn't really want to overcome. She told me that she wanted to make love to me just once before I got married and committed my life to her sister. I was in total shock and couldn't say a word.

She said, "I'm going upstairs to my bedroom, and if you want to go ahead with it just come up and get me." I was stunned. I was frozen in shock as I watched her go up the stairs. When she reached the top she pulled down her panties and threw them down the stairs at me. I stood there for a moment, then turned and went straight to the front door. I opened the door and stepped out of the house. I walked straight towards my car.

My future father-in-law was standing outside. With tears in his eyes he hugged me and said, "We are very happy that you have passed our little test.

We couldn't ask for a better man for our daughter. Welcome to the family."

The moral of this story is: always keep your condoms in your car.

Hunters

A 90-year-old man was having his annual checkup. The doctor asked him how he was feeling. "I've never been better," the old man replied. "I've got an eighteen-year-old bride who's pregnant and delivered a child. What is your opinion about that, Doc?" the old man asked.
The doctor thought for a moment, then says, "Well, let me tell you a story. I know a guy who is an hunter. He never misses a season for hunting.
But, one day he's in a bit of a hurry and he accidentally grabs his umbrella instead of his gun." The doctor continued, "So he's walking in the woods near a creek, and suddenly he spots a lion in some brush in front of him. He raises up his umbrella, points it at the lion and squeezes the handle.
BAM!!
The lion drops dead in front of him."
"That's impossible!" said the old man in disbelief. "Someone else must have shot that lion."
Exactly," said the Doctor.

Confessional

An old man walks into a confessional. The following conversation ensues:
Man: I am 92 years old, have a wonderful wife of 70 years, many children, grandchildren, and great grandchildren. Yesterday, I picked up two college girls, hitchhiking. We went to a motel, where I had sex with each of them three times.
Priest: Are you sorry for your sins?
Man: What sins?
Priest: What kind of a Catholic are you?
Man: I'm Jewish.
Priest: Why are you telling me all this?
Man: I'm telling everybody.

Embarrassing Medical Exams

1. A man comes into the ER and yells, "My wife's going to have her baby in the cab!" I grabbed my stuff, rushed out to the cab, lifted the lady's dress, and began to take off her underwear. Suddenly, I noticed that there were several cabs -- and I was in the wrong one.

Submitted by Dr. Mark MacDonald, San Antonio, TX.

2. At the beginning of my shift, I placed a stethoscope on an elderly and slightly deaf female patient's anterior chest wall. "Big breaths," I instructed. "Yes, they used to be," replied the patient.

Submitted by Dr. Richard Byrnes, Seattle, WA.

3. One day I had to be the bearer of bad news when I told a wife that her husband had died of a massive myocardial infarct. Not more than five minutes later, I heard her reporting to the rest of the family that he had died of a "massive internal fart."

Submitted by Dr. Susan Steinberg

4. During a patient's two week follow-up appointment with his cardiologist, he informed me, his doctor, that he was having trouble with one of his medications. "Which one?" I asked. "The patch, the nurse told me to put on a new one every six hours, and now I'm running out of places to put it!" I had him quickly undress, and discovered what I hoped I wouldn't see. Yes, the man had over fifty patches on his body! Now, the instructions include removal of the old patch before applying a new one.

Submitted by Dr. Rebecca St. Clair, Norfolk , VA.

5. While acquainting myself with a new elderly patient, I asked, "How long have you been bedridden?" After a look of complete confusion, she answered, "Why, not for about twenty years -- when my husband was alive."

Submitted by Dr. Steven Swanson, Corvallis , OR .

6. I was caring for a woman and asked, "So, how's your breakfast this morning?" "It's very good, except for the Kentucky Jelly. I can't seem to get used to the taste," the patient replied. I then asked to see the jelly, and the woman produced a foil packet labeled "KY Jelly."

Submitted by Dr. Leonard Kransdorf, Detroit , MI .

7. A nurse was on duty in the emergency room when a young woman with purple hair styled into a punk rocker mohawk, sporting a variety of tattoos, and wearing strange clothing, entered. It was quickly determined that the patient had acute appendicitis, so she was scheduled for immediate surgery. When she was completely disrobed on the operating table, the staff noticed that her pubic hair had been dyed green, and above it there was a tattoo that read, "Keep off the grass." Once the surgery was completed, the surgeon wrote a short note on the patient's dressing, which said, "Sorry, had to mow the lawn."

Submitted by RN, no name

AND FINALLY!!!...

8. As a new, young MD doing his residency in OB, I was quite embarrassed when performing female pelvic exams. To cover my embarrassment, I had unconsciously formed a habit of whistling softly. The middle-aged lady upon whom I was performing this exam suddenly burst out laughing and further embarrassing me. I looked up from my work and sheepishly said, "I'm sorry. Was I tickling you?" She replied, "No doctor, but the song you were whistling was, "I wish I was an Oscar Meyer Wiener."

Doctor wouldn't submit his name (Can't blame him!)

The funeral

One of the city's top cardiac specialists died. At his funeral, his coffin was placed in front of a huge replica of a heart made of red roses. When the pastor finished the sermon, and everyone said their good-byes, the large heart opened up, the coffin rolled inside, and the heart closed again. It was a majestic tribute to the much-loved cardiologist.
Suddenly, one of the mourners burst into a fit of laughter.
Irritated by his insensitivity, the man sitting next to him asked, "Why are you laughing, Mister?"
"I was just thinking about my own funeral," the man replied. "I'm a gynecologist."

Isolation

Tom had been in business for 25 years and was finally sick of the stress. He quit his job and bought 50 acres of land in Alaska as far from humanity as possible. He saw the postman once a week and got groceries once a month. Otherwise, it was total peace and quiet. After six months or so of total isolation, someone knocked on his door.
He opened it and there was a huge, bearded man standing there.
"Name's Lars, your neighbor from forty miles up the road. Having a Christmas party Friday night...thought you might like to come... about 5:00."
"Great," says Tom, "after six months out here I'm ready to meet some local folks. Thank you!"
Lars is leaving, he stops. "Gotta warn you...There's gonna be some drinkin'."
"Not a problem," says Tom. "After 25 years in business, I can drink with the best of 'em."
Again, as he starts to leave, Lars stops. "More 'n likely gonna be some fightin' too."
Tom says, "Well, I get along with people, I'll be alright. I'll be there. Thanks again."
Once again Lars turns from the door. "More 'n likely be some wild sex, too."
"Now that's really not a problem," says Tom, warming to the idea. "I've been all alone for six months! I'll definitely be there. By the way, what should I wear?"
Lars stops in the door again and says, "Whatever you want. Just gonna be the two of us."

Words of Wisdom

Two aliens landed in the Arizona desert near an abandoned gas station. They approached one of the gas pumps, and one of the aliens addressed it.

"Greetings, Earthling. We come in peace," said the younger of the two. "Take us to your leader."

The gas pump (of course) didn't respond. The younger alien looked cross, and the older one spotted this. "I wouldn't push it, if I were you," suggested the older one.

The younger creature ignored the warning and repeated the greeting. Again there was no response. Annoyed by what he perceived to be the pump's haughty attitude, he drew his ray gun, and said impatiently, "Greetings Earthling. We come in peace. Do not ignore us in this way! Take us to your leader, or I will fire!"

The older alien again warned his comrade, "You don't want to do that. You really don't want to make him mad!"

"Rubbish," replied the younger alien at his rapidly retreating comrade. He carefully aimed his weapon at the pump and fired.

There was a huge explosion. A massive fireball roared outwards and towards them and blew the younger alien off his feet and deposited him in a burnt and crumpled mess 200 yards into the desert.

Thirty-five Earth minutes later, when he finally regained consciousness, refocused his three eyes and straightened his bent antenna array, he looked dazedly up at the wiser one, who was standing over him, slowly shaking his big green head.

"What a ferocious creature," said the young, fried one. "It damn near killed us! How did you know it was so dangerous?"

The older alien leaned over, placed a friendly feeler onto the crispy one, and shared some knowledge...

"There's one thing I've learned during my travels through the galaxy," he said, "when a guy has a penis he can wrap around himself twice and then stick it in his own ear, … you don't mess with him."

Cover and back cover by GJEMB

www.ingramcontent.com/pod-product-compliance
Ingram Content Group UK Ltd.
Pitfield, Milton Keynes, MK11 3LW, UK
UKHW041836200726
13854UKWH00003BA/1168